The Civil War
Bawdy Houses
of
Washington, D.C.

Thomas P. Lowry, M.D.

—

Including a map of their former locations and a
reprint of the *Souvenir Sporting Guide* for the
Chicago, Illinois, G.A.R. 1895, Reunion.

Sergeant Kirkland's
Fredericksburg, VA

Published & Distributed by
Sergeant Kirkland's Museum
and Historical Society, Inc.
912 Lafayette Blvd., Fredericksburg, Virginia 22401-5617
Tel. (540) 899-5565; Fax: (540) 899-7643
E-mail: Civil-war@msn.com

Manufactured in the USA.
The paper in this book meets the guidelines for permanence and durability
of the Committee on Production Guidelines for Book Longevity
of the Council on Library Resources, Inc.

Library of Congress Cataloging-in-Publication Data

Lowry, Thomas P. (Thomas Power), 1932-
The Civil War Bawdy Houses of Washington, D.C.: including a map of their former locations and a reprint of
the Souvenir sporting guide for Chicago, Illinois, G.A.R.
1895 reunion / by Thomas P. Lowry.
    p.   cm.
Includes bibliographical references and index.
    ISBN 1-887901-14-0 (alk. Paper)
1. Prostitution – Washington (D.C.) – History – 19th century. 2. Soldiers – Washington (D.C.) – Sexual behavior –
History 19th century. 3. Sex customs – Washington (D.C.) –
History – 19th century. 4. United States – History -- Civil
War, 1861-1865 – Social aspects.
HQ146.W3L68   1997
975.3'02 – dc21   97-12519
                                               CIP

Printed in the United States of America.

Thomas P. Lowry, M.D., is a graduate of Stanford University, where he studied history and medicine. He has served in the U.S. Air Force and was on the staff of the Masters & Johnson Clinic in 1972 and 1973. His previous books and numerous journal articles are on anatomy and the history of medicine. For more than thirty-five years a physician and psychiatrist, Lowry is currently on the faculty of the University of California at San Francisco. His latest Civil War book, titled *The Story The Soldiers Wouldn't Tell: Sex in the Civil War* (1994), has received great interest and acclaim.

Other titles by Dr. Lowry include:

Hyperventilation and Hysteria: The Physiology and Psychology of Over Breathing and its Relationship to the Mind Body Problem. Compiled and edited by Thomas P. Lowry. With additional contributions by Edward H. Davis [and others] With a foreword by H. Corwin Hinshaw. Springfield, IL: C. C. Thomas [1967].

Camping Therapy: Its Uses in Psychiatry and Rehabilitation. Edited by Thomas Power Lowry, with seventeen additional contributors. With a foreword by Richard W. Hudgens. Springfield, IL: Thomas [1973, c1974].

The Story the Soldiers Wouldn't Tell: Sex in the Civil War / Thomas P. Lowry; with a foreword by Robert K. Krick. Mechanicsburg, PA: Stackpole Books, c1994.

The Attack on Taranto: Blueprint for Pearl Harbor / Thomas P. Lowry and John W. G. Wellham. Mechancisburg, PA: Stackpole Books, c1995.

CONTENTS

Chapter One

**Washington, D.C., During the Civil War
and its Bawdy Houses**   9

Chapter Two

**The Mapping of Washington, D.C.,
with Fold-out Map**   53

Chapter Three

The Grand Army of the Republic's
Souvenir Sporting Guide, **1895**   61

Index   95

Chapter One

Washington, D.C. During the Civil War and its Bawdy Houses

The Civil War was the first great conflict to be widely pictured by that new invention, the camera. France and England had led the way and, by 1860, daguerreotypes, ambrotypes, tintypes, cartes de visites and other formats of photographic representations were producing hundreds of thousands of images a year. North America was not far behind and photographic artists of every stripe soon thronged the great cities, or transported their cumbersome equipment in wagons to offer their services to rural populations.

After the fall of Fort Sumter, dozens of men rushed to record the gathering storm. Mathew Brady is the best-known of this legion, but dozens of equally skilled colleagues pointed their lenses at the War Between the States.

Everything seemed grist for the photographers' mill. Our archives are filled with images of politicians, authors, singers, actors, officers, cannons, steamboats, bombproofs, moats, bridges, parades, horses, canals, fortresses, opera houses, hotels, telegraph stations and semaphore operators. Privates, both Union and Confederate, posed by the tens of thousands, clutching bowie knives and revolvers, glowering with bellicosity.

In the representations of Washington, there are dozens of photos of the unfinished capitol dome and the even more embryonic Washington Monument, which was started in 1848, and completed in 1888. There are images of the original Smithsonian building and of balloon ascensions along the Mall. There would seem to be pictures of, literally, everything in the city – but such is not the case. The fifteen blocks between the White House and the Congress are almost totally unrecorded. There are a few parade scenes, vistas up Pennsylvania Avenue toward Capitol Hill, but the neighborhood itself astounds us by its absence.

It was hardly open fields with grazing cows. Every written description portrays it to be covered with buildings and teeming with life. Diaries, police reports and newspaper articles all confirm the area as being busy, night and day, with saloons, theaters, gambling dens, brothels, shops, small factories and surging crowds of off-duty or AWOL soldiers, who were evading the military police and looking for a good time.

"Hooker's Division," as the newspapers dubbed this area (it was also called Louse Alley and Murder Bay) had, in today's jargon, "non-stop action." And yet, from a photographic point of view, it might have never existed.

Why the absence? At least three possibilities loom. The first is that, with its throng of jostling crowds, the cameraman might lose his equipment to rowdies or thieves. The second possibility is the lack of a market. Who would buy photos of an illegal activity, one which a soldier would want to conceal from the folks at home? A corollary of this is the absence of the heroic. Images of a sad but noble President, a strutting George B. McClellan, a defiant David G. Farragut, a martyred Ephraim E. Ellsworth, all found patriotic customers. But a slattern poking her head out a second-story window? Not likely.

A third possible reason is human contempt for the familiar, enshrined in the cliché, "you don't miss it until it's gone." Why record the commonplace, the totally familiar? Even the photographers as recording angels, hoping to catalogue the vast panorama of the war, would hardly put Hooker's Division at the top of their lists.

Whatever the reason, a whole industry, an entire culture, is gone from our visual repositories. A thorough search of Federal, District of Columbia, and private archives has come up almost empty-handed. Certainly not a single photo is actually labeled as being a depiction of a bordello.

What we have done here, in this historical-archaeological re-creation, is to begin with the Provost Marshal's 1864, handwritten, address list of five dozen bordellos and place them onto the grid of streets existing at that time, using the house numbering system outlined in Boyd's Washington Directory of that same year. It is clear from the map that the densest concentration of doxies is around Pennsylvania Avenue, the very heart of America's political center.

Ninety years ago, reformers closed down Washington's houses of prostitution. The same trade exists today, of course, in call girls and street walkers, but the hidden nature of their activities today enables the self-appointed guardians of public morality to claim "victory."

But, from the actual historical record, stripped of "what should have been," it is clear that, during the Civil War, the prostitute trade existed openly, even brazenly, and formed an inescapable part of daily life in wartime Washington. We hope that, by providing these previously unacknowledged pieces of evidence of the social dimensions of the Civil War, we will have shed some light on the moral fabric of the time.

During the Lincoln administration, an adjacent neighborhood just south-east of the White House developed, saturated with vice, brothels, pickpockets, pimps, and low saloons. Today, it's known as the "Federal Triangle," with the Ronald Reagan Building, the Internal Revenue Service, and the Justice Department covering this area. We see the homeless, huddled over the warm air grates that ventilate the Metro subway. In the far distance, we may hear gunshots, as drug dealers murder their rivals as well as innocent bystanders. Government workers flee for the suburbs in the evening, and the prostitutes practice their trade in a dozen locations. (Library of Congress)

The head of the U.S. Secret Service, in 1864, was Colonel Lafayette C. Baker. His only previous police experience was that of having been a member of a San Francisco Vigilante Committee. However, he was able to make a name for himself by burning obscene literature seized from the mails, conducting raids on Washington's brothels, catching bounty-jumpers, and exposing crooked contractors. (National Archives, negative 111-B-1116)

Mathew Brady, who became famous for his photographs of the Civil War period, took his first view of the White House, or the President's home as it was then called, in 1861. The bronze statue of President Thomas Jefferson, a slave-holder, was later removed to the Rotunda in the Capitol where it can now be viewed. (National Park Service.)

Mathew Brady, sitting on the ground at the left, carefully carried his photographic equipment, including glass plates, in this outfit as he followed the Army from battlefield to battlefield. However, he neglected capturing the war between the sheets back home in Washington, DC. (National Archives)

Another famous Washington photographer was Alexander Gardner. His gallery was located at the corner of 7th and D Streets, as shown in this 1863 photograph, and it occupied the upper floors of the building. On the street-level floor was a sutler dealing in stationery. Just up D Street (right), in a four-story building at 396, was Robert Rainey's Hotel. Next to it, at 398 was Margruder, Beall & Co., dealing in boots and shoes. The nearby bawdy district was absent from his portfolio. (Library of Congress)

The Old City Hall at Judiciary Square, 4th and D Streets, NW, completed in 1858, stands out as a prominent example of Greek Revival architecture. The architect, George Hadfield, also designed the Curtis-Lee Mansion in Arlington, Virginia, and was, for a time, the supervising architect of the Capitol. Old City Hall has had many uses over the years – a slave market until 1862, a Civil War hospital, a patent office and a courthouse. Today, it houses the Superior Court of the District of Columbia. (Library of Congress)

The Military Provost Office kept "watch" over the various bawdy houses located throughout the city. Their register for 1864-65, follows, with an "Inmate" column, noting the number of women in each house. The 'Class' column, is an evaluation, with "1" as best, "2" as fair, "3" as poor, and "low" as bad.[1]

Bawdy Houses & Addresses	Inmates	Class
1. Miss Lucy Hart, *21 Pa. Ave.*	4	1
2. Madam Miller, *51 Pa. Ave.*	6	1
3. Mrs. Catharine Cambell, *138 24th St.*	5	2
4. Madam Bennett, *148 F St.*	7	?
5. Mrs. Louise Turner, *446 19th St. (?)*	5	1
6. Lizzie Miller, *corner 18th & E St.*	6	2
7. Mollie Turner, *62 C St.*	3	1
8. Hattie Farwell, *28 13½ St.*	2	2
9. Ellen Wolfe, *494 13 ½ St.*	4	3
10. Miss Mina Bowers, *478 13 ½ St.*	6	3
11. Mrs. Sarah Duncan, *474 13½ St.*	2	2
12. Miss Maggie Murphy, *282 D St.*	6	1
13. Sallie Murphy, *286 D St.*	6	1
14. Mary Taylor, *298 D St.*	6	low
15. Mollie Mason, *287 D St.*	7	1
16. Miss Joe Horn, *291 D St.*	7	2
17. Mrs. Mary Taylor, *305 D St.*	9	3
18. Mina Bearing, *309 D St.*	6	3
19. Miss Nichols, *591 12th St.*	5	1
20. Louie Myers, *533 12th St.*	4	2
21. Mrs. Louie Hays, *537 12th St.*	5	3
22. Miss Leote Gaskill, *541 12th St.*	6	1
23. Mrs. Louisa Koener, *540 12th St.*	5	3
24. Mrs. Maggie Walters, *532 12th St.*	14	1
25. Mrs. Louise South, *252 C St.*	6	2
26. John Sputsvists, *313 D St.*	6	low
27. Eliza Gibson, *531 11th St.*	House of Assignation[2]	
28. Miss Mollie Florence, *533 11th St.*	3	2
29. Miss Kate Walters, *595 11th St.*	3	2
30. Miss Mary Miller, *597 11th St.*	6	3
31. Mrs. Elizabeth Harrison, *284 C St.*	House of Assignation	
32. Miss Annie Wilson, *510 10th St.*	4	1
33. Miss Sophie Hoffman, *484 10th St.*	6	3
34. Mrs. E. M. Post, *487 10th St.*	6	1
35. Miss Nellie Gwinn, *348 E. St.*	4	1

[1] The original is handwritten and hard to read. See file number Vol. 298, RG 393, Provost Marshal, 22nd Army Corps, National Archives.

[2] Webster's: a lover's secret rendezvous; a lover's tryst.

36. Miss Jane Ross, *348 E St., back*	4	2
37. Sallie Austin, *500 6th St.*	9	1
38. Miss Julia Deen, *12 Marble Alley*	8	2
39. Miss Nelie Mathews, *10 Marble Alley*	6	2
40. Mrs. Elizabeth Harris, *33 Maine Ave., Island[3]*	9	2
41. Laura Tompkins, *225 B St., Island*	2	3
42. Mrs. J. Rhoades, *474 Maryland, Island*	6	very low
43. Mrs. E.M. Mark, *473 Maryland, Island*	2	very low
44. Mary Hall, *459 Maryland, Island*	18	1
45. Elizabeth Harley, *4 Maryland, Island*	3	1
46. Hattie Mills, *2nd near Maryland, Island*	3	3
47. Ann Benton, *Tin Cup Alley, Island*	5	3
48. Mary Hessler, *513 3rd St., Island*	5	3
49. Mary Murrey, *493 3rd St., Island*	6	very low
50. Miss Mary Donnelly, *339 C St., Island*	3	very low
51. Sarah Brown, *rear of 339 C St., Island*	5	very low
52. Margaret Wilson, *rear of 339 C St., Island*	3	very low
53. Mrs. Roland, *250 F St., Island*	4	4
54. Margaret Hanks, *Fighting Alley, Island*	6	low
55. Matilda Wade, *Fighting Alley, Island*	6	low
56. Mrs. Johnson, *640 7th St.*	3	low
57. Ellen Hall, *434 Virginia Ave., Island*	6	1
58. Mary Tolson, *G St., near 1st St., Island*	3	very low
59. Catharine Dinkloker, *4th @ N, near Navy Yard*	6	3
60. Rachael Rappider, *574 9th St., near H St.*	5	very low
61. Mary Conkin, *95 Pa. Ave., near 10th St.*	5	very low
62. Julia Fleet, *444 3rd St., Fox Hospital*	6	very low
63. Emaline Bateman, *N St., between 11th & 12th*	2	2
64. Margaret Venerable, *249 10th St.*	4	4
65. Louisa Sanford, *corner 3rd & L Sts.*	4	1
66. Eliza Foster, *rear N.J. Ave. & C St.*	1	3
67. Mary Jacobs, *rear N.J. Ave. & C St.*	1	3
68. Emma Howard, *rear N.J. Ave. & C St.*	5	3
69. Philamena Preston, *331 G St.*	3	3
70. Mrs. Weldon, *497 10th St., between G & H*	2	1
71. Mrs. Wiggons, *corner 1st & B St., Island*	6	very low
72. John Muntz, *512 N.J. Ave.*	*(not recorded)*	
73. Annie Jones, *195 Pa. Ave., near. 10th St.*	5	very low [4]

---

[3] "Island" refers to the area bounded by the canal and the Potomac River.
[4] In the preparation of the map, several of the original addresses, such as "Fighting Alley," proved impossible to locate, and those bordellos are not on the map. Further, the locatable 67 bawdy houses so crowd the map the "colored" houses were omitted. The reader can place most of them from the list on page 20.

Colored Bawdy Houses

Name and Address	Inmates	Class
1. Julia Thomas, *480 13th St.*	4	3
2. Two Houses, *rear of 348 E St.*	4	4
3. Misses Seal & Brown, *13 Marble Alley*	6	low
4. Theadosia Herbert, *Tin Cup Alley*	5	1
5. Rebecca Gaunt, *Tin Cup Alley*	4	2
6. Sarah Wallace, *Tin Cup Alley*	5	2
7. Sophia Harbour, *489 3rd St.*	2	1
8. Selia Higgins, *rear of 339 C St.*	5	2
9. Josaphine Webster, *Fighting Alley*	12	low
10. Biloy Becket, *243 E St., near 3rd St.*	5	low
11. Levinia Pergins, *352 Virginia Ave.*	3	2
12. Emily Brown, *H St., near 20th St.*	6	low

Cattle grazing on the "White Lot," so called because its fence was painted white. These military cattle yard and slaughter houses were adjacent to the Washington Monument grounds and the canal, now Constitution Avenue, Northwest, is seen in the foreground. The Treasury building and the outer limit of the bawdy district can be seen at the right. The White House can be seen in the upper center of the photograph. (Library of Congress)

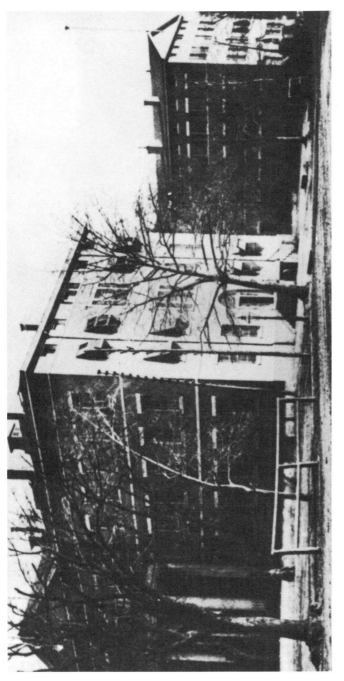

The War and Navy buildings bordering Pennsylvania Avenue as seen from Seventeenth Street, Northwest. The bawdy house of Annie Jones, (#73) was directly across the street from the War Department building and was rated "very low" by the Provost Marshal. This may be the same notorious Annie Jones who claimed romantic involvements with Franz Sigel, John E. Wool, George A. Custer, Judson Kilpatrick, and the superintendent of the Old Capital Prison. (Library of Congress)

The Metropolitan Hall Variety Theater was one of the several vaudeville venues near the bawdy district. The theater is flanked by The Washington Star newspaper offices on the left and a bakery on the right, at Eleventh Street and Pennsylvania Avenue. (Library of Congress)

This rare, 1874 photograph is the earliest known view of the lower section of 11ʳ Street, which once contained a dense segment of Washington's bawdy houses, during the Civil War. To the south, in the distance, rise the towers of the Smithsonian. Harvey's Oyster House stands on the left corner. To the right, along Pennsylvania Avenue, are the Latimer Cleary Auction House and Commission Merchants, The Washington Star Newspaper Building, and the Metropolitan Hall Theatre. (Smithsonian Institution)

This 1857 photo, taken on the block between 4th and 3rd Streets along Pennsylvania Avenue, looking east, shows the first row of columns being put in place in the drum of the Capitol's dome. If one turned left on 3rd Street, he would have found Tin Cup Alley just one block north, the haven for the bawdy house of Miss Ann Benton (#44), and her five ladies. (Office of the Architect of the Capitol)

The Surgeon General at Washington, D.C., began a collection of photographs documenting medical problems during the war. This unfortunate private is dying of the hideous effects of a particularly virulent case of syphilis. (Otis Historical Archives, National Museum of Health and Medicine, CP # 2141.)

The Reverend James C. Richmond, while in Washington, became attracted to Miss Rosa Bielaski, an inexperienced clerk,
who was newly-employed by the U.S. Government, at the
Treasury Building. Reverend Richmond showered her with re-
volting love letters and obscene notes. The Treasury Building
was situated just east of the White House and across the street
from the adjacent bawdy house district. Later in the war, Miss
Bielaski was discharged from her post, and Lincoln, who had
known her family in Illinois, interceded personally on her be-
half to restore her job. (Library of Congress, negative LC-USZ62-108021)

An example of the obscene letters written by the Reverend
Richmond to Miss Rosa Bielaski. This one was dated April 4,
1863, the same week Richmond met with President Abraham
Lincoln, in the White House, to tell him he (Richmond) was
"...driving the devil out of Washington." The bawdy houses
would stay; however, Richmond was forced to leave the capital, branded "lewd and wicked" by a fellow Army chaplain.
(National Archives, courtesy of Michael Musick and Howard Madaus.)

This rare photograph was taken from the United States Treasury Building looking south-east towards the Smithsonian Institute (upper left corner), and looking east along the outskirts of the bawdy house district, or along what some referred to as "Hooker's Division," a neighborhood of brothels and low saloons, of Washington. On this same south Treasury porch, the deranged Reverend James C. Richmond pressed his obscene drawings and verse into the hands of the unwilling Miss Rosa Bielaski. (Smithsonian Institute, negative 18603)

Treasury Department Building at Fifteenth Street and Pennsylvania Avenue, Northwest, showing the side entrance to the State Department Building (at right), later replaced by an extension of the Treasury. (Library of Congress)

Major General Joseph Hooker's name became associated with
the bawdy house district of Washington, D.C. Hooker's Army
of the Potomac headquarters was described as a combination
"barroom and brothel," by Charles Francis Adams, Jr., grand-
son of John Quincy Adams. (National Archives negative 111-B-3320)

This turn-of-the-century photograph is the earliest image found showing that which had been the bawdy district. Taken from the roof of the Smithsonian Building looking north-west, the Treasury can be seen just left of center, the White House to its left. The bawdy district would have occupied the foreground. (Library of Congress)

General view of the Potomac River looking toward Alexandria, Virginia, showing the unfinished Washington Monument, as sketched by Alfred R. Waud, a newspaper artist, from the roof of the Willard Hotel. The bar at the Willard was a center of intrigue and deal-making. Ambitious officers went there, seeking political allies who might secure for them higher rankings in their volunteer units. (Washington Evening Star)

Looking east on F Street, Northwest, towards the U.S. Patent Office building seen in the distance at left. Located on F Street was the bawdy house of Madam Bennett (#4), at number 148, with her seven girls. (National Park Service)

The old City Canal, described as a fetid bayou filled with floating dead cats, all kinds of putridity, and reeking with pestilential odors. This view was taken at the site of today's Reflecting Pool. The western portion of the canal ran through the site of today's Museum of Natural History. (National Park Service)

This is a telling photograph of the lock keeper's house at 17th Street at that which is now Constitution Avenue, ca. 1910. This stone house was built in 1832 at the junction of the C & O canal extension and the Washington City canal, which ran along the bawdy district. The canal has long been filled in by Constitution Avenue. This house still stands as a lone survivor of this era and its inhabitants. (Library of Congress)

Photo of Pennsylvania Ave., looking north-east along the outskirts of the bawdy district on the right side of the avenue. (Library of Congress)

This April, 1865, photograph of the Sanitary Commission storehouse and adjoining houses at 15th and F Sts., NW, shows the U.S. Treasury along 15th St., and hides the bawdy district, which began in the back yards of these row houses. (LC-B817-7709, glass, wet collodion)

This rare 1865 photograph of Haymarket Square at 9th Street and Louisiana (now Indiana) Avenue, NW, shows the Canterbury Theatre, which opened in 1821. The building at the left with the tower is the Central Guardhouse, behind which was the bawdy district. The Department of Justice now occupies this site. (Columbia Historical Society)

Trinity Episcopal Church, 3rd and C Streets, NW, ca. 1863. The design of the church, which stood from 1849 to 1936, was James Renwick's first plan, rejected as a proposed design for the Smithsonian Institution. The Gothic Revival church of red sandstone was attended by John C. Calhoun, Daniel Webster, Henry Clay and Francis Scott Key. When the Civil War broke out, the minister refused to read prayers for victory for the Union forces. He was fired. The Church was then seized by the Union and used as a hospital. The small building with the false front is William Birth's Grocery Store. To the right, one could find "Tin Cup Alley," the house of Ann Benton (#44) and her five girls, and a number of "Colored" bawdy houses. (Library of Congress)

This is a view looking north-west from the Senate Wing of the Capitol, 1861. This photograph was taken two months after the start of the Civil War and shows Pennsylvania Avenue (left) and the steeples of Trinity Episcopal Church, 3rd and C Streets, NW, (right foreground). This area between the Capitol and the White House was the oldest and most densely-settled portion of the city, with fine houses, inns, hotels, churches and public buildings. Only a few bawdy houses occupied this section. It was a quite different story on the other side of Pennsylvania Avenue. (Office of the Architect of the Capitol)

Northwest from the Capitol, June 27, 1861. New Jersey Avenue is at the right. A building marked "Depot House" in the center foreground stands in front of two trains of cars on the old Baltimore & Ohio Railroad tracks. Just up from these rails on New Jersey Avenue were the bawdy houses of Eliza Foster (#61), Mary Jacobs (#62), and Emma Howard (#63) and her five girls. (Fine Arts Commission)

Ford's Theater on 10th Street between E and F Streets, Northwest, showing the condition of the street and carriage-blocks used at entrances. The sign at the curb advertises Kimmel's Steam House. Various bawdy houses were located in this area, including Miss Annie Wilson (#32), Miss Sophie Hoffman (#33), Mrs. E. M. Post (#34), all on 10th Street. On E Street were Miss Nellie Gwinn (#35), and Miss Jane Ross (#36). (Library of Congress)

A rare panorama of Southwest Washington, August 18, 1863. The view, taken by Titian Ramsay Peale, from the central tower of the Smithsonian Building, shows Independence Avenue in the foreground, Virginia Avenue running diagonally, and 10th Street at the center, extending to the Potomac River waterfront. At the time, this area was closely built up with dwellings and commercial establishments. The Forrestal Building and L'Enfant Plaza occupy this area today. The only bawdy house recorded by the Provost's office in this general area was that of Mrs. Johnson (#51), located at 7th and E Streets, which would have been just off to the extreme left of this photograph. (Smithsonian Institution)

A rare panorama of Southwest Washington, August 18, 1863. A continuation of the Peale view shows at the center the intersection of Independence Avenue, Virginia Avenue and 12th Street. To the left of center is the Long Bridge over the Potomac to Virginia, exiting from Maryland Ave. It was near Maryland Ave. on 11th St., that one could find the bawdy houses of Miss Kate Walters (#27) and her 3 ladies, as well as Miss Mary Miller (#28) and her 6 ladies. Closer to the Smithsonian grounds (right corner) one could find the bawdy house of Miss Nichols (#17) and her 5 ladies. The masts of ships are visible to the left of the bridge. (Library of Congress)

A rare photograph of Maine Avenue looking northeast, April, 1865. At that time, Maine Avenue ran diagonally from 4th to 6th Streets, SW, through what is now the Mall. The white frame building beyond the brick residences has a sign over the sidewalk proclaiming it to be the business of Thomas Somerville & Robert Leitch, brass founders and ironworkers. One of Washington's larger bawdy houses stood on this avenue, and belonged to Mrs. Elizabeth Harris (#38) and her nine ladies. (Library of Congress)

B Street South (now Independence Avenue) and 12th Street, SE, looking north-east, 1863. This photo by Mathew Brady shows the Smithsonian building and the Mall. The Smithsonian grounds were the first area of the Mall to be landscaped, beginning in 1849, while the building was under construction. The informal design incorporated 150 species of trees and shrubs. On 12th Street near this corner was the bawdy house of Miss Nichols (#17) and her five ladies. (Library of Congress)

This 1862 photograph by A. J. Russell of the Smithsonian Institution shows the sharp contrast between a certain elegance and the conditions that many of the working class of Washington labored under. (Library of Congress)

This rare 1880 photograph shows the Washington slave pens, which stood in the alley behind G Street, between 4½ and 6th Streets, NW. Until 1862, Washington was a center for domestic slave trading. The city served as a depot for the purchase of interstate traders, who combed Maryland and Northern Virginia for slaves. The pens were torn down in 1889. (Library of Congress)

On October 9, 1863, Titian R. Peale photographed Columbus Scriber, a free black, and a dealer in flour and feed, both wholesale and retail, at 119 E Street, SW. The "Colored" bawdy house of Biloy Becket was nearby with its 5 ladies, and the bawdy house known as "Two Houses" could be found in the rear of 348 E Street with its 4 ladies. (Columbia Historical Society)

Bird's-eye view of 6th Street wharf where military supplies were received. Sixth Street was also the location of Miss Sallie Austin's bawdy house (#37), with its nine girls, which received a number one rating from the Provost Marshal's office. (Library of Congress)

Map showing the defenses of Washington. (National Park Service)

Chapter Two

The Mapping of Washington, D.C.

As the war began, perhaps the most vulnerable area of the Union was the nation's capitol. Situated on the banks of the Potomac River, Washington, D.C., was located between the Commonwealth of Virginia, which ratified the ordinance of secession on April 17, 1861, and Maryland, which initially wavered but remained a part of the Union. On the evening of May 23, as soon as sufficient troops were on hand in the nation's capital, Federal regiments crossed the Potomac into Virginia and began occupying the strategic approaches to the city. Within the next two months, efforts were concentrated on the preparation of earthen fortifications to defend the city from an attack from the South. Throughout the war, the defenses of Washington were extended, strengthened, and modified. Entrusted with this important task was Brevet Major General John G. Barnard of the Corps of Engineers. General Barnard served as Chief Engineer of the Army of the Potomac, from 1861 to 1862; Chief Engineer of the Department of Washington from 1861 to 1864; and then as Chief Engineer of the armies in the field from 1864 to 1865. In his *Report on the Defenses of Washington*, published after the war, Barnard noted with some pride that:

> From a few isolated works covering bridges or commanding a few especially important points, was developed a connected system of fortication by which every prominent point, at intervals of 800 to 1,000 yards, was occupied by an enclosed field-fort, every important approach or depression of ground, unseen from the forts, swept by a battery for field-guns, and the whole connected by rifle-trenches which were in fact lines of infantry parapet, furnishing emplacement for two ranks of

men and affording covered communication along the
line, while roads were opened wherever necessary, so
that troops and artillery could be moved rapidly from
one point of the immense periphery to another, or under
cover, from point to point along the line.[5]

Of the numerous maps depicting the defense of Washington,
D.C., the detailed map complied by the U.S. Army Corps of Engineers showing the entire interlinking network of fortifications is
of particular importance. Measuring 132 by 144 centimeters, this
remarkable map was made to accompany General Barnard's offi-
cial report on the defenses of the nation's capital. Albert Boschke's
notable 1861 printed map of Washington, D.C., was used as the
base, and to it army map-makers added, by hand, cultural data on
Virginia, a new map title, forts, batteries, and the rifle pits, as well
as the military roads to link them.

General Barnard's remarkable system of fortifications suc-
cessfully protected the capital from external enemies, but was of
little use against more subtle enemies boring from within. Neither
cannon nor parapet nor abatis defended men against a sidelong
glance, or the thrilling touch of a feminine hand, or the musical
tones of a Southern voice, proffering notions that swelled male
pride. The name of Greenhow invokes the mythic and legendary
powers ascribed to some women.

Rose O'Neal Greenhow was born in Montgomery County,
Maryland in 1817, and, in 1861, resided in a three-story brick
building, #398, on 16th Street, just north of the White House. She
was a leader in Washington society, a passionate secessionist, and
one of the most renowned spies in the Civil War for the Confederate cause. She was credited by President Jefferson Davis as
helping win the battle of 1st Manassas with the information she
sent to General Pierre G. T. Beauregard.

Although beyond proof, considerable circumstantial evidence
linked Rose Greenhow with Senator Henry Wilson, powerful
chairman of the Committee on Military Affairs, devoted aboli-
tionist, author of the post-war Freedmen's Bureau legislation, and
future Vice-President. In spite of his absolute devotion to the Fed-

---

[5] U.S. Army Crops of Engineers, *Report on the Defenses of Washington to the Chief of Engineers, U.S. Army, by Bvt. Maj. Gen. J. G. Barnard* (Washington: Government Printing Office,
1871), 33.

eral cause, he seems to have spent many unaccounted-for hours in privacy with Mrs. Greenhow, and may have inadvertently provided the information for which Davis was so grateful.

After her arrest as a spy, she was placed under guard at her home, which was then called "Fort Greenough." On November 17 1861, Greenhow wrote Secretary of State William H. Seward, stating,

> You have held me sir, to man's accountability, and I therefore claim the right to speak on subjects usually considered beyond a women's ken, and which you may class as 'errors of opinion.' I offer no excuse for this long digression, as a three months' imprisonment, without formula of law, gives me authority for occupying even the precious moments of a Secretary of State. My object is to call your attention to the fact: that during this long imprisonment, I am yet ignorant of the causes of my arrest; that my house has been seized and converted into a prison by the Government; that the valuable furniture it contained has been abused and destroyed; that during some periods of my imprisonment I suffered greatly for want of proper and sufficient food. Also, I have complaint that, more recently, a woman of bad character, recognized as having been seen on the streets of Chicago as such, by several of the guard, called herself Mrs. Onderdonk, was placed here in my house, in a room adjoining mine... The 'iron heel of power' may keep down, but it cannot crush out, the spirit of resistance in a people armed for the defense of their right; and I tell you now, sir, that you are standing over a crater, whose smothered fires in a moment may burst forth. It is your boast, that thirty-three bristling fortifications now surround Washington. The fortifications of Paris did not protect Louis Phillippe when his hour had come.[6]

Shortly afterward, Greenhow was moved to the Old Capitol Prison. Months later, she was released, and sent to Richmond, Virginia.

---

[6] Richmond, VA: Richmond Whig.

Mrs. Rose O'Neal Greenhow (1814-1863), (the aunt of Mrs. Stephen Douglas), had a home opposite St. John's Church in view
of the White House. The "beautiful rebel of Sixteenth Street,"
and her daughter were photographed in the courtyard of the
Old Capitol Prison after protesting her "house arrest." (Library of
Congress)

Washington, D.C. The Old Capitol Prison, 1st and A Streets NE. Today it's the site of the U.S. Supreme Court. When Annie Jones was imprisoned here, she claimed to have seduced three of the male staff members. (Library of Congress-B815-1019, glass, wet collodion.)

"Secesh" women leaving Washington for Richmond, Virginia. At that time the Washington police conducted a "house cleaning," sending south various women, including Greenhow and her daughter, as well as various female "residents" from the local bawdy ward. "GRAND EXODUS OF FEMALES RICHMOND-WARD," reported the press. "Among Cyprians thus 'swarming-off' from the hives are delegations from various noted establishments about town: *Sal Austin's, No. 10 Marble Alley, The Iron-Clad Battery, Fort Sumter, The Monitor, Headquarters U.S.A.; Gentle Annie Lyles,* and *The Cottage By The Sea.*" (Library of Congress)

Fold-Out Map of Washington, D.C.

Chapter Three

The Grand Army of the Republic's *Souvenir Sporting Guide,* 1895

The most powerful veteran's organization in the history of the United States was the Grand Army of the Republic. Known best as the GAR, it was organized by Union veterans in 1866.

The GAR served many purposes. It drew veterans together for purposes of nostalgia and reminiscence. The members spoke of their shared joys and sorrows, of memories in camp and combat. They assured each other that their sufferings and sacrifices had been for noble purposes. They honored fallen comrades. They refought the tactics and strategies of every battle in a thousand meetings, in formal sessions and, less formally, over many a glass of shared refreshment.

One of their functions would be, in today's jargon, as a support group. The term Post-Traumatic Stress Disorder had not yet been invented, but the mental damage of combat is ever the same. The veterans of Viet Nam, a war of often obscure purpose, returned home to have their doubts and fears further enhanced by denunciations from their "peace-loving" fellow citizens, who treated the soldiers as pariahs. The Civil War soldier could find his healing not only in the parades and memorial speeches, but in frequent convivial gatherings with his comrades in arms. They knew the same songs, had suffered the same illnesses, had heard the same Minie balls whistle past (and sometimes into) their bodies.

As they aged, their nostalgia increased, the old war wounds ached more, and kindly recollections of comradeship seemed to replace the painful memories of shattered bodies and amputating surgeons. A particularly poignant remembrance of things past were the lyrics of J. M. Carmichael, a Confederate soldier of the 15th Alabama Infantry, in his song *Long Ago*. In its recorded form, sung by Bobby Horton, it elicits a tear from all but the most jaded eye. Carmichael speaks of youth, but goes on to reflect, "But now we are aged and gray, comrades, trials of life are nearly done..." The song evokes the touching films made of the last reunions at Gettysburg, during the early administration of Franklin D. Roosevelt. Old men in blue and gray, their beards long and white, posed for the camera, some erect and unbowed, some on crutches, some in wheelchairs.

But whatever the frailties of these veterans in the 1930s, in the late 1800s, they were a powerful political force. At its peak, in 1890, the GAR had over 400,000 members, and exerted a profound influence on the Republican party until the end of the nineteenth century. Through their influence with the White House and the Congress, the GAR created a very favorable political climate for Civil War veterans, their widows and their orphans. The Pension Bureau grew into a vast bureaucracy and an army of examining physicians evaluated the flood of claims. Frequent pension increases saw to the welfare of the Union veteran.

Today, Memorial Day is commemorated by the Indy 500 and traffic problems, but, in 1868, when that holiday was brought into being by GAR influence in Congress, it truly was memorial. Families decorated the graves of their fallen loved ones and politicians waxed eloquent upon the sacrifices of those who had died to save the Union.

The GAR had a vast web of local and regional chapters, but, for many members, the high point was the national convention. There were, of course, the usual prayers and songs, the dedication of monuments and memorials, the scurrying of office-seekers, and an efflorescence of oratory.

But, like conventioneers of most other groups and eras, they liked to have a good time.

It was traditional for some enterprising publicist in most host cities to publish a *Sporting Guide*. While this usually included race tracks, velodromes, and other places of amusement, the majority of space was given up to the advertisements of bordellos.

As always, there is much to be learned from the study of history, and the muse Cleo has not disappointed us here. In the current era of tabloids, scandal reporters and paparazzi who follow nearly everyone of public prominence and, when some sexual irregularity is detected and forced upon the public, learned pundits pontificate, moralists bewail our crumbling social fabric, and the extroverted, professional, finger-pointers of the clergy, weaned on teleprompters, computerized mailings, and fifty-dollar haircuts, appear on the tube to warn us of spiritual decay, and the need to cleanse our nation and return instantly to family values.

What is apparent in the sporting guide of the past is that none of the advertisers seem burdened with shame or self-loathing. Sexual behavior, for money, is portrayed as an ordinary transaction, to mutual benefit. The message is: boys far from home will enjoy a little action, and then board the train. No harm done. (This, of course, overlooks the problem of venereal disease in the era before penicillin.) And what did the GAR wives think of this? We are not told. Perhaps it was like the Army policy on homosexuality: "Don't ask; don't tell."

Now, should these GAR members who might have succumbed to the delights promised in this guide be seen as men simply carried away by the indiscretions of youth? A glance at the year of the convention shows that, by the simplest arithmetic, these GAR men were mostly in their fifties, some much older. Many were portly, with graying whiskers, and were prosperous, cigar-smoking Republicans, yet they were seen as a ready audience by the madams who placed these ads.

What is the reader to think of this guide? It is only a way to consider the era and the audience and to have, if only for a moment, a glimpse into a world now gone.

❧G. A. R.❧

Souvenir

Sporting

Guide.

WENTWORTH PUBLISHING HOUSE, PRINTERS,
1895

3

PHŒNIX HILL PARK.

Special Attractions for

G. A. R. Week:

Bradt's National War Museum,

Open Day and Night.

Take Green Street line of Cars to Entrance,

Fountain Ferry Park.

Finest Record-Breaking Bicycle Track in the World.

SID BLACK, Champion trick rider of world, will give exhibitions daily. Also, **BENNER BROS.,** of **Philadelphia,** juvenile cyclists, aged 4 and 6 years, exhibiting the smallest tandem in the world.

Take West-bound Market Street Cars direct to entrance without transfer.

4

RIVERSIDE PARK

JOHN KESSLER, Manager.

G. A. R. WEEK:

**Bicycle Racing, Balloon Ascensions, Dancing
And Other Amusements.**

Take west-bound Green street cars marked
Parkland or **Riverside.**

☞Nice 5-Mile Ride.

NATIONAL PARK.

—

Special
Attractions **G. A. R. Week.**
For

Take Main Street Line West.

Macauley's Theater. Week Commencing SEPT. 9,

AL. G. FIELD'S MINSTRELS

Will hold the boards at this popular house
for one week.

Walnut, Near Fourth St.

5

AVENUE THEATER. Week commencing Sept. 9,

"A CRACKER JACK" COMPANY

Will·amuse the patrons during

G. A. R. WEEK.

Fourth Avenue, Bet. Green and Walnut.

GRAND OPERA HOUSE.

Week Commencing Sept. 9.

The Great War Drama,

"SHENANDOAH,"

Will recall the memory of old Vets to the late unpleasantness, as well as interest the rising generation.   'Tis highly staged.

Jefferson, Bet Second and Third Sts.

BUCKINGHAM THEATER,

Week Commencing SEPT. 9.

THE HOME OF VAUDEVILLE.

Continuous Performance

From I P. M. Until II P. M.

Jefferson St., Bet. Third and Fourth.

6

BESSIE DEAN

616 Green Street.

Visitors to the city during the race meet-
ing and G. A. R. Encampment should not
fail to pay **Miss Bessie Dean** a visit. Miss
DEAN has one of the most commodious
houses, not only in this city, but any city
in the country, and for fineness and beauty
the interior cannot be excelled. At Miss
Dean's, which is at 6:6 Green street, can
be found 14 of the most charming young
ladies to assist visitors in making life one
continuous round of pleasure during their
stay.

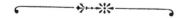

Finest Brands
      of Wines
            in the Market.

7

JEW LOUIE,

612 Green Street.

Very, very plain; nothing suggestive to strangers about the name or place of residence, but the amount of meaning conveyed by that name and address to her friends, who are legion, is sufficient to insure her a well filled house throughout the Encampment. She is one of the very few women of her nationality in the country that owns and conducts such an establishment. Miss Louie is a typical Jewess, and while not related to the Baron across the pond, one would think from the Oriental splendor in which her house is furnished from pit to dome that she had free access to his millions. Miss Louie has 12 of the most accomplished young ladies in the city from the East to assist her in receiving her callers, any one of whom can perform exceedingly well upon the piano, and among them are several vocalists of no mean ability.

Finest Brands of Wine and Beer.

8

HATTIE LAWRENCE,

630 TENTH ST.,

—AND—

633 WEST ST.

Owing to her increasing popularity, it has been absolutely necessary for MISS HATTIE to open the large mansion at 630 Tenth street, which she has done at an enormous expense. She also continues the management of the cozy little cottage at 633 West street. MISS HATTIE being endowed with true Kentucky hospitality has rightly gained the distinction of being one of the most liberal entertainers in the South, she having donated liberally to the G. A. R. fund, being ample proof of her liberality. She has twelve of the prettiest young ladies in the South to entertain her visitors. She also keeps the best brands of Wine and Beer.

9

DAISY MILLS,

711 West Street,

Bet. Madison and Walnut, 10th and 11th.

To the many visitors to the city during the Encampment and Races the writer desires to call their especial attention to the delightful little cottage owned and personally managed by Miss DAISY. Miss DAISY is deserving of a crowded house throughout the Encampment, as she has converted her house from an exclusively private into a public one during that period. She has four of her most intimate friends from Chicago to assist her in receiving her callers, and as they are all beautiful and accomplished, it is unnecessary to add they are the swellest of swell entertainers.

She also keeps the
Choicest Brands of Wine and Beer.

10

LOTTIE CLARE,

631 West Street,

Bet. Tenth and Eleventh and Walnut and Grayson.

———————

This beautiful house is presided over by
one of the most unique and clever entertainers in the South, and as it is strictly
first-class and private she caters to nothing
but the very fashionable set. To the fast
set of the upper crust of society gents is
this invitation extended. MISS LOTTIE
keeps the choicest brands of

WINE and BEER.

II

FANNIE EVANS,

603 WEST ST.

FIRST=CLASS.

FRIENDS CALL.

Strangers Cordially Invited.

Mary Edwards,

732 Green Street.

To the people that pay this city periodical visits MISS MARY needs no introduction,
as those that visit her beautiful palace are
so highly entertained that they are sure to
pay her a return visit as often as they
come to the city. She has a host of beautiful ladies who are excellent entertainers
to assist her in making life well worth liv-
ing to visitors to the Encampment and
Races. Finest brands of Wine and Beer,

12

ELSIE ✸ LIVINGSTON,

828 Grayson Street.

    While out seeing the sights, boys, do not fail to drop in upon MISS ELSIE at the above number, and you will be royally entertained. Everything and everybody connected with her establishment is first-class. She has the following named ladies to entertain you:

Misses Freddie,
Annie,
Edna,
Alice,
Blanche,
Marie,
Grace.

    MIss ELSIE is an Ohio girl and will be pleased to see all visitors from home.

She has a fine line of

Wine and Beer,

13

❧HALLIE REED,❧

824 Grayson St.

—❧⋯❊⋯—

Visitors to the Encampment and Races will not make their visit complete if they fail to pay Miss HATTIE a visit. She has just opened the above number and has a corps of pretty girls to entertain callers.

She also keeps the choices brands of Wine and Beer.

Georgia Stewart,

830 Grayson Street.

As there are only a few first-class houses upon this street, and as the Guide only contains the names of first-class resorts it will therefore be the duty of the writer to devote a space to the above-named lady. She is a clever and liberal entertainer and has a number of beautiful girls to assist her to entertain her callers.

She also has a fine line of Wine and Beer.

14

Mad. La Roy,

626 TENTH ST.

❉❉❉❉❉❉❉

VISITORS to the Encampment will miss
a grand treat if they fail to pay the
Madame and her famous beauties a
visit. MAD. LA ROY is the only lady of
her nationality in any of the Western cities
that own and conduct a palace such as
the one owned and personally managed by
herself. Her ladies being mostly of the
same nationality, combined with the elegance of the furnishings and the swell
manner in which they entertain callers,
makes the Madame's one of the most popular of the many resorts in the city.

❉❉❉❉❉❉❉

She also keeps

THE CHOICEST BRANDS OF

WINES AND BEER.

15

Maggie Blakemore,

620 Tenth Street.

❧•◐◑•❧

ALL visitors that are sportively inclined can have their inclination gratified by merely dropping into MISS B.'s cozy little castle. It is a veritable little palace, and with Miss MAGGIE as the Queen and her bevy of beauties as Princesses Americans that have not crossed the pond nor visited the royalty can easily imagine themselves as being before the throne. MISS B. is located at 620 Tenth street, and will be pleased to renew old and form new acquaintances during the encampment. She has ten ladies to entertain callers.

❧•◐◑•❧

Finest Wines and Beer.

16

Minnie Ward.

623 Tenth Street,

Has Handsomely
—————Furnished

PRIVATE APARTMENTS

—— TO LET——

To Married Men Only.

Mother Mack,

325 Eleventh Street.

This well-known lady is exceedingly
popular with the sporting fraternity, who
all know her liberal manner of entertaining. She keeps a strictly first-class resort at the above number, and cordially in-
vites all perusers of this Guide to call. She
has a number of beautiful ladies to entertain her callers.

Finest brands of Wine and Beer.

17

Mollie Glover,

710 Hancock Street.

AS has been stated before in this Guide to the visitors in search of sport, it is not confined to a certain street or locality as in other cities provided the house is first-class and orderly. MISS GLOVER prides herself upon having a strictly first-class resort at 710 Hancock street, where visitors can enjoy themselves hugely if they are in quest of sport. She has ten of the most beautiful young ladies in the South to entertain her visitors.

She also keeps the choicest brands of

Wines and Beer.

18

Anna Neurietter,

714 Hancock Street.

Miss ANNA has one of the most attractive
establishments in the city, and visitors to
the Encampment and Races are hereby extended a cordial invitation to call. She
has eight beautiful and pleasing young
ladies to entertain callers.

She also keeps the finest brands of Wine
and Beer.

STELLA SCHMELZ,

720 Green Street.

To many of the visitors to the city to the
Encampment who in the past have paid
periodical visits to Cincinnati this name is
very familiar, as Miss STELLA conducted a
house there for some years. She has recently reopened the above number, and
everything and everybody is new and first-
class. She has eight beautiful girls to entertain her callers.

She also has the finest brands of Wine
and Beer.

19

Fannie Clark,

408 Jackson Street.

MISS FANNIE conducts one of the most exclusive establishments in the city and she has quite a number of young and beautiful ladies to assist her in entertaining her numerous friends as well as visitors to the Encampment and Races. She also keeps a fine assortment of Wines and Beer.

Minnie Grant,

410 Jackson Street.

As there are only a limited number of first-class resorts on this street, and as the writer only advertises the strictly first-class resorts, it therefore makes it its duty to devote a space to this popular proprietress. She is not only a clever entertainer but has surrounded herself with six pleasing young ladies that wilt assist her to entertain friends and visitors to the Encampment and races. She has a fine line of Wines and Beer.

20

LIZZIE LONG,

123 East Green Street.

MISS LIZZIE HAS ALWAYS CONducted one of those quiet rooming houses, but owing to the fact that so many of her friends will be here to attend the Races and Encampment and having such a large, roomy house, she has decided to convert it into a public house during that time. Her parlors will be graced with some of Cincinnati's famous beauties that are here on pleasure bent, and visitors will be entertained in a royal manner. She keeps the choicest brands of Wine and Beer.

21

Maud Shively,

722 Green Street.

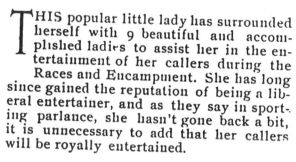

THIS popular little lady has surrounded herself with 9 beautiful and accomplished ladies to assist her in the entertainment of her callers during the Races and Encampment. She has long since gained the reputation of being a liberal entertainer, and as they say in sporting parlance, she hasn't gone back a bit, it is unnecessary to add that her callers will be royally entertained.

She also keeps the finest brands of

Wine and Beer.

22

MOLLIE McCORMICK,

1027 Madison Street.

TO THE many "married" people that visit the city during the Encampment it will be rather difficult for them to enjoy the comforts and privacy of home in their cramped quarters at the various hotels, boarding and lodging houses. The writer wishes to inform visitors that Miss MOLLIE conducts an exclusively first-class private rooming house at the above number, and they may enjoy all the privileges of a well-kept home in her parlors.

She also keeps the _____

Choicest Brands of Wine and Beer.

23

FANNIE HILLMAN.

712 and 714 GREEN STREET.

THIS large double mansion is presided over by one of the most popular and liberal entertainers in the city. She has fourteen handsome young ladies to enter her callers during the Races and Encampment. She also keeps the finest brands of

WINE AND BEER.

24

Blanche Griswold

611 Green Street.

THIS popular and pleasing little lady having recently retired from business, and being urgently requested by an army of admiring friends to reopen an establishment, did so upon the 14th of August, and having surrounded herself with an even dozen of beautiful ladies to entertain her callers, combined with the furnishings, which are all new and expensive from cellar to garret, should make her place one of the most popular to visitors to the city during the Encampment.

Finest Brands of Wine and Beer

25

Kittie Ward,

215 Ninth Street,

THIS large three-story mansion is the only strictly first-class resort on this street. Miss KITTIE has a wide circle of friends throughout the country, and to those that have not visited her since she has been in her present location, and also visitors to the Encampment and Races, she hereby extends a cordial invitation to call. She has 14 handsome ladies to entertain visitors.

She also keeps the Choicest Brands

Of Wine and Beer.

26

SIGNORETTA ALFARETA,

642 GREEN STREET.

This large mansion is presided over by one of the most liberal entertainers of her race in the south. She has surrounded herself with twenty-one famous Spanish beauties, and as they are all beautiful and accomplished, beyond a doubt her parlors will be taxed to their utmost capacity. Her parlors are furnished elegantly and with rare taste. In fact, the Oriental splendor in which they are furnished is enough to dazzle the eyes of many who have visited the royal palaces abroad. Visitors that are in search of amusement should not fail to pay this palace a visit for they will be entertained royally, as among the ladies are several rare vocalists, good musicians and dancers. She also keeps choice brands of Wine and Beer.

27

CREOLE.

Sallie Scott,

624 and 626

Green.

Northern visitors to the Encampment have no doubt heard of the famous Creole Beauties to be seen south of the Mason and Dixon line. Miss Scott has surrounded herself with 28 famous Creole beauties to assist her in the eatertainment of her callers during that period. She has gathered these ladies from all the principal cities of the Sunny South, and used rare judgment in selecting them, for not only their beauty of face and form, but also for their intellectual and social attainments, conspicuous among them being that far-famed Creole beauty, Miss Rhoda Nord. To her many friends throughout the country that peruse this Guide Miss Sallie hereby extends an invitation to call when in the city.

28

CREOLE.

KATE PAYNE,

640 GREEN STREET.

ONE of the handsomest and best ap-
pointed houses in the city is the
one that is presided over by
MISS KATE at the above number.
It has the reputation of being one of the
finest in the South, and between the fine
furnishings and the fair occupants of this
strictly first-class resort it will surely re-
ceive the patronage of the high-toned visitors to the Encampment and Races. She
has eighteen of the most beautiful Creole
beauties ever gotten together under one
roof, and as there are good singers, dancers
and musicians among them, visitors have
the assurance that they will be highly entertained. She also has the finest brands
of

Wine and Beer.

29

Wentworth's Souvenir Sporting Guides

Have been published in the following cities:

Chicago, World's Fair,
New Orleans, Mardi Gras,
Frisco Midwinter Fair,
Memphis Spring Races.

Will be gotten out in Atlanta for the Cotton States Exposition, also Dallas for the fight.

Index

1

1st St. 19
3rd St. 19, 20, 25
6th St. 19, 46, 49, 51
7th St. 19
9th St. 18, 19, 39
10th St. 18, 19, 43, 44
11th St. 18, 23, 24
12th St. 18, 45, 47
13 ½ St. 18
13th St. 20
15th St. 30, 38
16th St. 54, 56
17th St. 22, 36
20th St. 20
24th St. 18

A

A Street 57
Adams, Charles F., Jr. 31
Adams, John Q. 31
Alabama, 15th Infantry 62
Alexandria, VA 33
Alfareta, Signoretta, Chicago, IL .. 90
Alice, Miss, Chicago, IL 76
Annie, Miss, Chicago, IL 76
Arlington, Virginia 17
Army of the Potomac 31
Austin, Sallie 19, 51
Avenue Theater, Chicago, IL 69

B

B Street South 19, 47
Baker, Lafayette C. 13

Balloon Ascensions, Chicago, IL 68
Baltimore & Ohio Railroad 42
Barnard, John G. 53
Bateman, Emaline 19
Bawdy house district 27, 29
Bearing, Mina 18
Beauregard, Pierre G. T. 54
Becket, Biloy 20
Benner Bros. , Chicago, IL 67
Bennett, Madam 18, 34
Benton, Ann 19, 25, 40
Bicycle Racing, Chicago, IL 67, 68
Bielaski, Rosa 27, 28, 29
Blakemore, Maggie, Chicago, IL .. 79
Blanche, Miss, Chicago, IL 76
Boschke, Albert 54
Bowers, Mina 18
Boyd's Washington Directory 11
Bradt's National War Museum,
   Chicago, IL 67
Brady, Mathew 9, 14, 15, 47
Brothels 12, 13
Brown, Emily 20
Brown, Miss 20
Brown, Sarah 19
Buckingham Theater, Chicago, IL 69

C

C & O Canal 36
C Street 18, 19, 20, 40, 41
Calhoun, John C. 40
Cambell, Catharine 18
Canterbury Theatre 39
Capitol 25, 41, 42
Carmichael, J. M. 62
Cattle 21
Central Guardhouse 39
City Canal 35
Civil War hospital 17

Clare, Lottie, Chicago, IL.............74
Clark, Fannie, Chicago, IL............83
Clay, Henry.................................40
Colored Bawdy Houses................20
Congress 2, 10, 12, 21, 22, 27, 43, 46,
    47, 48, 49, 51, 56, 58, 62
Conkin, Mary...............................19
Constitutional Ave. 21, 36
Cottage By The Sea, The 58
Cotton States Exposition, Atlanta.93
Cracker Jack Co. , Chicago, IL 69
Crayson St., Chicago, IL 77
Creole beauties.........................91, 92
Curtis-Lee Mansion........................17
Custer, George A. 22

D

D Street 16-18
Dallas, TX 93
Davis, Jefferson................................54
Dean, Bessie, Chicago, IL 70
Deen, Julia 19
Department of Justice 39
Depot House 42
Dinkloker, Catharine 19
Domestic slave trading 49
Donnelly, Mary...............................19
Douglas, Stephen............................56
Duncan, Sarah................................18

E

E Street 18, 19, 20, 43, 44, 50
Edna, Miss, Chicago, IL.................76
Edwards, Mary, Chicago, IL.........75
Eleventh St., Chicago, IL..........74, 80
Ellsworth, Ephraim E.....................10
Evans, Fannie, Chicago, IL ,
    Chicago, IL..................................75

F

F Street 18, 19, 34, 38, 43
Farragut, Daivd G. 10
Farwell, Hattie 18
Federal Triangle.............................12
Field's, Al. G.....................................68
Fighting Alley..............................19, 20
Fleet, Julia 19
Florence, Mollie 18
Ford's Theater.................................43
Forrestal Building...........................44
Fort Greenough..............................55
Fort Sumter..................................9, 58
Fortification 53
Foster, Eliza................................19, 42
Fountain Ferry Park, Chicago, IL.67
Fourth Ave. , Chicago, IL 69
Freddie...76

G

G Street..19, 49
GAR....................................61, 62, 63
Gardner, Alexander 16
Gaskill, Leote 18
Gaunt, Rebecca 20
Gentle Annie Lyles............................58
Gibson, Eliza 18
Glover, Mollie, Chicago, IL...........81
Grace, Miss, Chicago, IL................76
Grand Army of the Republic 61
Grand Opea House, Chicago, IL ..69
Grant, Minnie, Chicago, IL............83
Grayson St., Chicago, IL 76, 77
Greek Revival architecture............17
Green St., Chicago, IL 70, 71, 75, 82,
    84, 85, 87, 88, 90-92
Greenhow, Rose O..............54, 56, 58
Griswold, Blanche, Chicago, IL....88
Gryson St., Chicago, IL 74
Gwinn, Nellie............................18, 43

H

H St.. 19, 20
Hadfield, George............................ 17
Hall, Ellen...................................... 19
Hall, Mary...................................... 19
Hancock St., Chicago, IL 81, 82
Hanks, Margaret 19
Harbour, Sophia............................ 20
Harley, Elizabeth........................... 19
Harris, Elizabeth 19, 46
Harrison, Elizabeth 18
Hart, Lucy 18
Harvey's Oyster House 24
Haymarket Square 39
Hays, Louie..................................... 18
Headquarters U.S.A 58
Herbert, Theadosia 20
Hessler, Mary 19
Higgins, Selia................................. 20
Hillman, Fannie, Chicago, IL........ 87
Hoffman, Sophie 18, 43
Homeless... 12
Hooker, Joseph 31
Hooker's Division 10, 29
Horn, Joe 18
Horton, Bobby 62
Howard, Emma...................... 19, 42

I

Independence Avenue....... 44, 45, 47
Indiana Avenue.............................. 39
Internal Revenue Service............... 12
Iron-Clad Battery, The..................... 58
Island 19

J

Jackson St., Chicago, IL 83
Jacobs, Mary.......................... 19, 42
Jefferson St., Chicago, IL 69
Jefferson, Thomas.......................... 14

Johnson, Mrs............................ 19, 44
Jones, Annie 19, 22, 57
Judiciary Square 17
Justice Department........................ 12

K

Kessler, John 68
Key, Francis S. 40
Kilpatrick, Judson 22
Kimmel's Stream House............... 43
Koener, Louisa............................... 18

L

L'Enfant Plaza 44
La Roy, Mad. , Chicago, IL 78
Latimer Cleary Auction House 24
Lawrence, Hattie, Chicago, IL......72
Leitch, Robert................................. 46
Lincoln, Abraham 28
Livingston, Elsie, Chicago, IL.......76
Lock keeper's house...................... 36
Long Ago 62
Long Bridge 45
Long, Lizzie, Chicago, IL 84
Louie, Jew, Chicago, IL................. 71
Louisiana Avenue 39

M

Macauley's Theater, Chicago, IL ..68
Mack, Mother, Chicago, IL 80
Madison St., Chicago, IL 73, 86
Maine Ave. 19
Maine Avenue 46
Mall... 47
Manassas, 1st 54
Marble Alley 19, 20
Marble Alley, No. 10 58
Margruder, Beall & Co. 16
Marie, Miss, Chicago, IL 76
Mark, E. M., Mrs. 19

Market Street Cars, Chicago, IL 67
Maryland 49, 53
Maryland Ave................................45
Mason, Mollie 18
Mathews, Nelie...............................19
McClellan, George B. 10
McCormick, Mollie, Chicago, IL ..86
Medical Department 32
Memorial Day 62
Wentworth's Souvenir Sporting
   Guides: Chicago, World's Fair;
   New Orleans, Mardi Gras; Frisco
   Midwinter Fair 93
Metro subway 12
Metropolitan Hall Theatre 23, 24
Miller, Lizzie 18
Miller, Madam 18
Miller, Mary 18, 45
Mills, Daisy, Chicago, IL 73
Mills, Hattie...................................19
Minstrels 68
Monitor, The 58
Montgomery County, MD.............54
Muntz, John....................................19
Murphy, Maggie.............................18
Murphy, Sallie 18
Murrey, Mary..................................19
Museum of Natural History ...35, 36
Myers, Louie 18

N

N St..19
National Park, Chicago, IL............68
Navy Yard.......................................19
Neurietter, Anna, Chicago, IL 82
New Jersey Avenue.................19, 42
Nichols, Miss.....................18, 45, 47
Ninth St., Chicago, IL....................89
Nord, Rhoda, Chicago, IL 91

O

Old Capitol Prison........22, 55, 56, 57

Old City Hall..................................17
Onderdonk, Mrs. 55

P

Patent Office...................................17
Payne, Kate, Chicago, IL...............92
Peale, Titian R. 44, 45, 50
Penicillin...63
Pennsylvania Ave. 10, 11, 18, 19, 22-
   25, 30, 37, 41
Pension Bureau 62
Pergins, Levinia 20
Phillippe, Louis..............................55
Phoenix Hill Park, Chicago, IL 67
Pickpockets.....................................12
Pimps 12
Post, E. M., Mrs..........................18, 43
Post-Traumatic Stress Disorder....61
Potomac River..............33, 44, 45, 53
Preston, Philamena.........................19
Provost Marshal....................11, 22

R

Rappider, Rachael 19
Reed, Hallie, Chicago, IL..............77
Reflecting Pool 35
Renwick, James...............................40
Report on the Defenses of Washington
  53
Rhoades, J., Mrs. 19
Richmond, James C. 27-29
Richmond, Virginia.................55, 58
Riverside Park, Chicago, IL...........68
Robert Rainey's Hotel 16
Roland, Mrs.....................................19
Ronald Reagan Building................12
Roosevelt, Franklin D. 62
Ross, Jane....................................19, 43
Russell, A. J.....................................48

S

Sal Austin's 58
Saloons.. 12
San Francisco Vigilante Committee
.... 13
Sanford, Louisa 19
Sanitary Commission storehouse 38
Schmelz, Stella, Chicago, IL.......... 82
Scott, Sallie, Chicago, IL 91
Scriber, Columbus.......................... 50
Seal, Miss....................................... 20
Senate Wing 41
Seward, William H........................ 55
Shenandoah.................................... 69
Shively, Maud, Chicago, IL 85
Sid Black.. 67
Sigel, Franz.................................... 22
Slave pens...................................... 49
Slaves 49
Smithsonian 24, 29, 44, 40, 45, 47, 48
Somerville, Thomas 46
South, Louise 18
Sputsvists, John 18
St. John's Church............................ 56
Star Newspaper.............................. 24
State Department Building 30
Stewart, Georgia, Chicago, IL....... 77
Superior Court, District of
    Columbia 17
Surgeon General............................ 26
Syphilis.. 26

T

Taylor, Mary 18
Tenth St., Chicago, IL ...72, 74, 78-80
Third St., Chicago, IL...................... 69
Thomas, Julia 20
Tin Cup Alley 19, 20, 25, 40
Tolson, Mary.................................. 19
Tompkins, Laura 19
Treasury Building 21, 27, 29, 30
Trinity Episcopal Church........ 40, 41

Turner, Lousie 18
Turner, Mollie................................ 18

U

U.S. Army Corps of Engineers 54
U.S. Patent Office 34
U.S. Secret Service 13
U.S. Supreme Court 57
U.S. Treasury 38

V

Vaudeville...................................... 69
Venerable, Margaret 19
Venereal disease............................ 63
Vice.. 12
Virginia.. 45
Virginia Ave. 19, 20
Virginia Avenue...................... 44, 45

W

Wade, Matilda 19
Wallace, Sarah 20
Walnut St., Chicago, IL 68, 69, 73, 74
Walters, Kate............................. 18, 45
Walters, Maggie 18
War Department building.............. 22
Ward, Kittie, Chicago, IL............... 89
Ward, Minnie, Chicago, IL............ 80
Washington City canal 35, 36
Washington defenses..................... 52
Washington Monument 9, 21, 33
Washington Star newspaper 23
Waud, Alfred R. 33
Webster, Daniel 40
Webster, Josaphine......................... 20
Weldon, Mrs. 19
West St., Chicago, IL 72-75
White House   10, 12, 14, 27, 28, 41,
    54, 56, 62
    President's home 14

White Lot..21

Wiggons, Mrs...................................19

Willard Hotel 33

William Birth's Grocery Store.......40

Wilson, Annie 18, 43

Wilson, Margaret............................19

Wolfe, Ellen......................................18

Wool, John E.....................................22